Fundamentals Of Investments In U.S. Financial Markets,
<u>Study Guide</u>

Fundamentals Of Investments In U.S. Financial Markets,
<u>Study Guide</u>

A comprehensive educational
resource for gaining knowledge and
understand of investments in
the U.S. financial markets.

Jack D. Howell Jr.

The American Institute
For Financial Education

Published in the United States of America by:

The American Institute
For Financial Education

4920 Roswell Road, Suite 45B-508
Atlanta, GA. 30342

Library of Congress Catalog Card Number: Applied

Howell, Jack D., Jr.
   Fundamentals of Investments In U.S. Financial Markets, Study Guide:

   1. Investments. 2. Retirement Planning. 3. Stocks. 4. Bonds
   5. Detailed Questions and Answers with Explanations

ISBN 0-9668050-1-1

"This publication is designed to provide accurate and authoritative information in regard to the subject matter covered. It is sold with the understanding that the publishers not engaged in rendering legal, accounting, or other professional service. If legal advice or expert assistance is required, the services of a professional person should be sought."
-*From a Declaration of Principles jointly adopted by a Committee of the American Bar Association and a Committee of the Publishers and Associations.*

Artwork by Romerofisk and AIFE ………………………..   Atlanta, Georgia

Printed in the United States of America   1st Edition

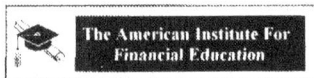

Fundamentals of Investments in U.S. Financial Markets

Study Guide

The study of investments is not dissimilar to the study of any other subject. The student must not only absorb the basic concepts of the material, but also acquire the ability to apply the concepts to real world applications. This point is vital. The study of investments and investment principals without the practice of real world implementation, renders the study itself useless. This study guide attempts to help bridge the divide between theoretical concepts and practical usefulness.

As with any new subject, vocabulary is paramount. Understanding the meaning of words employed in the study of a subject is a prerequisite to understanding the particular subject. Because new academic knowledge is primarily vocabulary driven, the text this study guide refers to, *Fundamentals of Investments in U.S. Financial Markets* by Howell is designed in a manner that highlights new words, phrases, and concepts in an effort to aid the learning process.

This study guide is intended for use as a supplement to the textbook. It is also intended to aid the individual as he or she moves through the material. The subject matter is presented in an organized manner that incorporates continuity with repetition. The study guide chapters bear the same titles and order as the textbook chapters, and summarize the essential concepts from the corresponding textbook chapter. This gives the readers more than one perspective on each topic and, hopefully, enhances the readers understanding of the material.

The user should read the chapter in the textbook first, then study the corresponding chapter within the study guide. Answers with explanations are given in a separate section. One should bear in mind that in some instances more than one answer may seem appropriate, it is left to the reader to determine which answer is "most" appropriate.

Chapter 1 Review Course

1) Stock:

       A) Represents money an investor has loaned to a corporation?
       B) Represents money a corporation has loaned to an investor?
       C) Represents an ownership interest in a corporation?
       D) None of the above.

2) Stocks are sometimes called:

       A) Debt Securities
       B) Equity Securities
       C) Male Securities
       D) Female Securities

3) Shares of stock actually trading in the marketplace are called:

       A) Authorized Shares
       B) Issued Shares
       C) Outstanding shares
       D) Treasury Shares

4) Common shareholders have the right to:

       A) Inspect the records of the company
       B) Freely transfer ownership
       C) Pro rata share of dividends or other distributions
       D) All of the above

5) If a shareholder wishes to vote on a corporate action but is unable to attend the annual meeting, the vote can be submitted via a:

       A) Voters Request Form
       B) Substitute Voters Form
       C) Absentee Ballot
       D) Proxy

6) When shares are held in a brokerage account, those shares are said to be held in:

       A) Brokers Name
       B) Customers Name
       C) Street Name
       D) Primary Holders Name

7) The Transfer Agent is responsible for:

    A) Canceling old shares and issuing new shares:
    B) Maintaining an accurate and updated record of all shareholders
    C) Mailing corporate information to shareholders
    D) All of the above

8) When a company pays out a portion of its profits to shareholders, this payment is called a:

    A) Profit sharing Payment
    B) Interest Payment
    C) Equity Payment
    D) Dividend Payment
    E) None of the above

9) Which is true of American Depository Receipts:

    A) Securities representing ownership in Foreign Stocks
    B) Securities traded on U.S. Stock Exchanges
    C) Securities registered with U.S. regulators
    D) Securities that have no voting rights
    E) All of the above

10) Which security is not an equity security:

    A) Warrant
    B) Stock
    C) Right
    D) Debenture
    E) American Depository Receipt

11) Which of the following is untrue with regard to Preferred Stocks:

    A) It is an equity security
    B) It has a prior claim on corporation assets
    C) It pays a fixed interest rate
    D) Its price does not fluctuate

12) The terms cumulative, convertible, callable, and participating are primarily used in relation with:

    A) Debt securities
    B) Equity securities
    C) Common stocks
    D) Preferred stocks

Chapter 2 Review Course

1) Bonds are a type of:

   A) Equity Security
   B) Option Security
   C) ADR Security
   D) Debt Security

2) Which of the following is <u>not</u> a major issuer of bonds?

   A) Corporations
   B) Individuals
   C) Local Governments
   D) State Governments
   E) Federal Government

3) The term "book entry" means the security:

   A) Is not represented by a physical certificate
   B) Is kept in a book
   C) Is recorded in a computer database only
   D) Is an entry on all government records
   E) A & C only

4) A "coupon" represents the bonds:

   A) Term
   B) Length
   C) Interest rate
   D) Face Value

5) A "Zero-Coupon" bond would:

   A) Pay no interest
   B) Have a short term
   C) Have a Zero face value
   D) Expire shortly

6) What is the relationship between bonds and interest rates:

    A) Bond prices decline when interest rates rise
    B) Bond prices rise when interest rates rise
    C) Bond prices decline when interest rates fall
    D) Bond prices rise when interest rates fall
    E) A & D
    F) B & C
    G) None of the above

7) Which is not a type of bond yield:

    A) Current Yield
    B) Nominal Yield
    C) Absolute Yield
    D) Yield to Maturity

8) Which is not a type of bond "risk":

    A) Call Risk
    B) Liquidity Risk
    C) Interest Rate Risk
    D) Legislative Risk
    E) Maturity Risk

9) Which represents the largest bond issuer:

    A) Federal Government
    B) State Government
    C) Corporations
    D) Local Governments

10) Which is not a Government fixed income security:

    A) Treasury Note
    B) Treasury Bill
    C) Treasury Letter
    D) Treasury Bond

11) The Federal government allows certain companies to have the first opportunity to purchase government securities, these companies are called:

    A) Primary Dealers
    B) Secondary Dealers
    C) First Choice Dealers
    D) Preference Dealers

12) Bonds issued by local and state governments are called:

  A) Government Bonds
  B) State Bonds
  C) City Bonds
  D) Municipal Bonds

13) A bond whose interest and principle are payable to the person who possess the bond is called:

  A) Adjudicated Bond
  B) Holder Bond
  C) Fully Registered Bond
  D) Bearer Bond

14) Which is not a type of Municipal Bond:

  A) Revenue Bond
  B) General Obligation Bond
  C) Short Term Notes
  D) City Bonds

15) Which bond type does not obligate the holder to pay federal taxes:

  A) Municipal Bonds
  B) Government Bonds
  C) Corporate bonds
  D) State Bonds

16) Which bond type may enable the investor to pay no local, state, or federal taxes on interest received:

  A) Government bond
  B) Corporate Bond
  C) Municipal Bond
  E) State Bond
  F) First Choice Dealers
  G) Preference Dealers

17) In order to analyze the effects of tax-free interest on bond yields, the investor should be familiar with:

  A) Tax-Free Equivalent yields
  B) Tax Equivalent Yield
  C) Taxable yields
  D) All of the above

18) Treasury Bills have a maturity of:

    A) 1 year or less
    B) 1 to 5 years
    C) 5 to 10 years
    D) All of the above

19) Treasury Notes have a maturity of:

    A) 1 year or less
    B) 1 to 10 years
    C) 5 to 10 years
    D) Over ten years

20) Treasury Bonds have a maturity of:

    A) 1 to 5 years
    B) 5 to 10 years
    C) 10 to 30 years
    D) Over 30 years

21) All Municipal issues must be reviewed by an attorney, the attorney gives what is called:

    A) A legal review
    B) A legal description
    C) A legal opinion
    D) A legal determination

22) The best type of review the attorney can give is called:

    A) Qualified
    B) Unqualified
    C) Satisfactory
    D) Complete

23) Which is untrue of Municipal Bond trading:

    A) Trading is very light
    B) Trading is very heavy
    C) All trades take place in the Over-The-Counter market
    D) A good quote is called a "firm" bid

Chapter 3 Review Course

1) Money Market securities are:

    A) Fixed income securities
    B) Equity Securities
    C) Debt Securities
    D) A & C
    E) None of the above

2) All money market instruments mature in:

    A) 90 Days
    B) 5 Years or less
    C) 1 Year or less
    D) 10 Years or less
    E) None of the above

3) Most Money Market instruments:

    A) Are issued at discounts
    B) Pay no interest
    C) Are considered extremely safe
    D) All of the above
    E) None of the above

4) Which of the following may be money market instruments:

    A) Treasury Bills
    B) Treasury Notes
    C) Treasury Bonds
    D) Commercial Paper
    E) Certificates of Deposits
    F) All of the above
    G) None of the above

5) Money Market instruments are considered:

    A) Very safe
    B) Moderately safe
    C) Moderately risky
    D) Very risky

Chapter 4 Review Course

1) A mutual fund is technically a:

   A) Face Amount Certificate Company
   B) Unit Investment Trust
   C) Management Company
   D) Collaborative Company

2) Which is not a type of mutual fund:

   A) Open End
   B) Short Term
   C) Closed End

3) An Open End fund has how many shares outstanding:

   A) 1 million
   B) Over 5 million
   C) Over 100 million
   D) Unlimited

4) Closed End funds have how many shares outstanding:

   A) 1 million
   B) Over 5 million
   C) Over 100 million
   D) Specified at time of issuance

5) The company responsible for bringing the fund "public" is called:

   A) Investment advisor
   B) Custodian Broker
   C) Investment manager
   D) Fund Sponsor

6) The document which specifies all the details of the fund is called the:

   A) Legal description
   B) Fund description
   C) Prospectus
   D) Detail information sheet

7) Mutual funds provide many benefits to investors. Which is not a commonly recognized benefit of mutual funds:

    A) Investment affordability
    B) Diversification
    C) Riskless investments
    D) Professional management

8) Which is not a type of mutual fund:

    A) Growth fund
    B) Income fund
    C) Balanced fund
    D) Specialized fund
    E) None of the above

9) Open End funds trade on an exchange:

    A) True
    B) False

10) Closed End funds trade on an exchange:

    A) True
    B) False

11) When the purchase of a mutual fund includes a sale charge, the fund is called:

    A) No Load fund
    B) Loaded fund
    C) Fee Fund
    D) Commission Fund

12) When the purchase of a mutual fund does not include a sale charge, the fund is called:

    A) No Load Fund
    B) Loaded Fund
    C) No-Fee Fund
    D) No-Commission Fund

13) Net Asset Value is the method of pricing for:

    A) Closed End funds
    B) Asset Funds
    C) Income Funds
    D) Open End Funds

14) The purchase price of a Closed End Mutual Fund is determined:

      A) Immediately
      B) At days end
      C) At tomorrow's ending price
      D) At the week's ending price

15) The purchase price of an Open End Mutual Fund is determined:

      A) Immediately
      B) At days end
      C) At tomorrow's ending price
      D) At the week's ending price
      E) Possibly B & C
      F) None of the above

16) Which would not be considered primarily a mutual fund company:

      A) Fidelity
      B) Templeton
      C) Vanguard
      D) Merrill Lynch
      E) Putnam

17) A mutual fund company offering many different funds is said to have an

      A) Variety
      B) Fund aggragate
      C) Fund family
      D) Fund collection

18) Which would not be a typical mutual fund expense:

      A) Management fee
      B) Brokerage fee
      C) Printing fee
      D) Plant & equipment fee

Chapter 5 Review Course

1) Most securities trade in which market(s):

    A) Primary market
    B) First market
    C) Secondary market
    D) Both A & B
    E) Both A & C
    F) Both B & C
    G) None of the above

2) Stocks listed on the NYSE trade in the:

    A) Primary market
    B) Secondary market
    C) First market
    D) Both A & B
    E) Both A & C
    F) Both B & C

3) When a stock is issued as an "IPO", it is first traded in the:

    A) Primary market
    B) Secondary market
    C) First market
    D) Both A & B
    E) Both A & C
    F) None of the above

4) Existing securities are traded in which market:

    A) Primary market
    B) Secondary market
    C) First market
    D) Both A & B
    E) Both A & C
    F) None of the above

5) Trades that are executed on the NASD are trading in which market:

    A) Primary market
    B) First market
    C) Second market
    D) Secondary market
    E) None of the above

6) Listed securities that are executed "off the floor" are trading in the:

    A) First market
    B) Primary market
    C) Second market
    D) Fourth market
    E) None of the above

7) An individual who works for an exchange, and is responsible for keeping an "orderly" market is called a:

    A) Specialist
    B) Market maker
    C) Floor trader
    D) Auctioneer
    E) None of the above

8) A stockbrokerage firm which executes trades for clients only is called a:

    A) Broker
    B) Specialist
    C) Dealer
    D) Client Dealer
    E) None of the above

9) A stockbrokerage firm which executes trades for itself only is called a:

    A) Broker
    B) Specialist
    C) Dealer
    D) Firm Dealer
    E) None of the above

10) A stockbrokerage firm which only executes trades for clients though other brokers charges a :

    A) Mark-up
    B) Settlement fee
    C) Commission
    D) Transfer fee
    E) None of the above

11) A stockbrokerage firm which executes trades out of its own inventory charges a:

    A) Mark-up
    B) Settlement fee
    C) Commission
    D) Transfer fee
    E) None of the above

12) An individual who trades in the NASDAQ market, and is responsible for keeping an "orderly" market is called a:

    A) Specialist
    B) Market maker
    C) Floor trader
    D) Auctioneer
    E) None of the above

13) When placing an order to purchase securities immediately, at the current price, you are placing a:

    A) Immediate order
    B) Market order
    C) Limit order
    D) "Or better" order
    E) None of the above

14) When placing an order to purchase or sell at a specific price, you are placing a:

    A) Immediate order
    B) Market order
    C) Limit order
    E) "Or better" order
    F) None of the above

15) When placing an order to sell below the current trading price, you are placing a:

       A) Market order
       B) Limit order
       C) Stop order
       D) Sell specific order
       E) None of the above

16) An order that will expire if not executed during the current trading session is a:

       A) Market order
       B) Limit order
       C) Day order
       D) GTC order
       E) None of the above

17) An order that will not expire until executed is a:

       A) Market order
       B) Limit order
       C) Day order
       D) GTC order
       E) None of the above

18) An order to buy or sell at any price at the beginning of the trading day is a:

       A) Market order
       B) Limit order
       C) GTC order
       D) Market on Open order
       E) None of the above
       F) A & D

19) An order to buy or sell at any price, but only at the end of the trading day is a:

       A) Market order
       B) Limit order
       C) GTC order
       D) End-of-Day order
       E) None of the above

20) An order to sell securities you do not own is called a:

    A) Market order
    B) Sell specific order
    C) Short sell order
    D) Limit sell order
    E) None of the above

21) A brokerage firm that gives investment advice is called a:

    A) Full service firm
    B) Half service firm
    C) Advice firm
    D) Assistance firm
    E) None of the above

22) A brokerage firm that does not give investment advice is called a:

    A) Full service firm
    B) Half service firm
    C) Non-advice firm
    D) Discount brokerage firm
    E) None of the above

23) A brokerage firm that does not give investment advice and also offers extremely low commissions is called a:

    A) Full service firm
    B) Low service firm
    C) Discount brokerage firm
    D) Deep discount brokerage firm
    E) None of the above

Chapter 6 Review Course

1) When purchasing securities on "margin", you are:

    A) Loaning securities
    B) Buying securities with cash
    C) Borrowing money
    D) Lending money
    E) None of the above

2) When purchasing on margin, shares are registered in:

    A) Buyers name
    B) Bankers name
    C) Avenue name
    D) Street name
    E) None of the above

3) The amount which an investor must repay the brokerage firm is the:

    A) Credit balance
    B) Loanable balance
    C) Market balance
    D) Debit balance
    E) None of the above

4) The total value of securities in a margin account is the:

    A) Total Value
    B) Indexed Value
    C) Current Market Value
    D) Firm Market Value
    E) None of the above

5) The amount of account value owned by the account holder is termed:

    A) Credit balance
    B) Debit balance
    C) Current market value
    D) Equity
    E) None of the above

6) The regulation which governs margin loan rates is called:

    A) Regulation A
    B) Regulation 43
    C) Regulation T
    D) Regulation M
    E) None of the above

7) After purchasing securities on margin, if the current market value drops to a certain level the brokerage firm will ask for an additional funds deposit, this request is termed a:

    A) Federal request
    B) Equity Call
    C) Maintenance Call
    D) Funds Call
    E) None of the above

8) By using a margin account, an investor is able to purchase more securities, this ability is referred to as:

    A) Purchasing Power
    B) Buying Power
    C) Capital Power
    D) Borrowing Power
    E) None of the above

9) In order for investors to avail themselves to margin, the account must be funded with a minimum of:

    A) $5,000.00
    B) $10,000.00
    C) $1,000.00
    D) $2,000.00
    E) $2,500.00
    F) Any amount

Chapter 7 Review Course

1) Securities analysis is used as a means of measuring and controlling:

    A) Prices
    B) Cost
    C) Inventory
    D) Risk
    E) None of the above

2) An event that would have a negative impact on all securities is called:

    A) Systematic Risk
    B) Market Risk
    C) Unsystematic Risk
    D) Both A & B
    E) None of the above

3) An event that might have a negative impact on just one security is called:

    A) Systematic Risk
    B) Market Risk
    C) Unsystematic Risk
    D) Business Risk
    E) Both C & D
    F) None of the above

4) The type of analysis which seeks to determine "which" security to buy is:

    A) Technical analysis
    B) Buy side analysis
    C) Fundamental analysis
    D) Algorithm analysis
    E) None of the above

5) All of the following are financial statements except:

    A) Income statement
    B) Balance sheet
    C) Statement of changes to retained earnings
    D) Statement of retained assets
    E) None of the above

6) Assets minus liabilities equals:

    A) Net Capitalization
    B) Net Depreciation
    C) Gross Capitalization
    D) Net Worth
    E) None of the above

7) Current assets minus current liabilities equals:

    A) Net Capitalization
    B) Net Depreciation
    C) Gross Capitalization
    D) Working Capital
    E) None of the above

8) The value assigned to a company after all assets have been liquidated and all liabilities have been paid is termed:

    A) Liquidated Value
    B) Firm Value
    C) Net residual Value
    D) Book Value
    E) None of the above

9) A corporations profit margin measures the:

    A) Amount of profit per dollar of sales
    B) Amount of profit per dollar of assets
    C) Amount of profit per dollar of capitalization
    D) Amount of profit per dollar of dividends
    E) None of the above

10) Return on assets measures the corporations:

    A) Percentage gain on inventory
    B) Percentage gain on securities
    C) Percentage gain on expenses
    D) Percentage income on assets
    E) None of the above

11) Cash flow represents how much "cash" is flowing through:

   A) The corporations bank account
   B) The corporations stock price
   C) The corporations accounts receivables
   D) The corporation after financial obligations for current period
   E) None of the above

12) Earnings Per Share represents the amount of corporate income:

   A) On a capitalized basis
   B) On a debt/equity basis
   C) On a accrual basis
   D) On a per common share basis
   E) None of the above

13) Technical analyst are sometimes referred to as:

   A) Saucers
   B) Chartist
   C) Techno crats
   D) Techni-researchers
   E) None of the above

14) When a security's price is moving steadily higher, it is said to be in a:

   A) Consolidation pattern
   B) Resistance pattern
   C) Uptrend pattern
   D) Ascending pattern
   E) None of the above

15) When a security's price is moving steadily lower, it is said to be in a :

   A) Consolidation pattern
   B) Resistance pattern
   C) Downtrend pattern
   D) Descending pattern
   E) None of the above

16) When a security's price goes significantly above or below its trading range:

    A) A "pop-through" has occurred
    B) A "consolidation" has occurred
    C) A "new-beginning" has occurred
    D) A "breakout" has occurred
    E) None of the above

17) An average calculation which adds a new point while removing the oldest point is:

    A) A "rolling" average
    B) A "sliding" average
    C) An "adjustable" average
    D) A "moving" average
    E) None of the above

18) When markets are moving steadily and strongly, they are said to have:

    A) Staying power
    B) Positive movement
    C) Discretionary movement
    D) Momentum
    E) None of the above

19) The "beta" of a stock measures the:

    A) Vulnerability of the security in relation to itself
    B) Volume of the security in relation to past volume
    C) Pricing of the security as it relates to past pricing
    D) Risk of the security as it relates to the overall market
    E) None of the above

Chapter 8 Review Course

1) Which of the following is not a part of the business cycle:

    A) Expansion
    B) Prosperity
    C) Recession
    D) Recovery
    E) Depression
    F) None of the above

2) When the U.S. Congress enacts an economic package, this is an example of:

    A) Fiscal Policy
    B) Monetary Policy
    C) Keynesian Policy
    D) Liberal Policy
    E) None of the above

3) When the Federal Reserve raises or lowers interest rates, this is an example of:

    A) Fiscal Policy
    B) Monetary Policy
    C) Keynesian Policy
    D) Conservative Policy
    E) None of the above

4) When prices are rising and economic output is constant, the economy is experiencing:

    A) Prosperity
    B) Recession
    C) Deflation
    D) Inflation
    E) None of the above

5) When prices are falling and economic output is constant, the economy is experiencing:

    A) Prosperity
    B) Recession
    C) Inflation
    D) Deflation
    E) None of the above

6) The tool which measures prices as they relate to an individual is called:

    A) Real price index
    B) Producer price index
    C) Individual price index
    D) Consumer price index
    E) None of the above

7) The tool which measures prices as they relate to businesses is called:

    A) Productivity price index
    B) Real price index
    C) Manufacturing price index
    D) Producer price index
    E) None of the above

8) Real interest rates measure the percentage return after:

    A) Inflation
    B) Deflation
    C) Risk
    D) Productivity
    E) None of the above

9) Of all the interest rates the Federal Reserve may adjust, which has the most impact on the U.S. economy?

    A) Prime rate
    B) Broker call rate
    C) Fed funds rate
    D) Discount rate
    E) None of the above

10) Which is not a function of the Federal Reserve:

    A) Adjusting interest rates
    B) Adjusting the money supply
    C) Regulating the banking industry
    D) Conducting open market operations
    E) None of the above

11) Which is not a business cycle indicator:

    A) Leading economic indicators
    B) Lagging economic indicators
    C) Coincident economic indicators
    D) Adjunct economic indicator
    E) None of the above

12) When a country, as a whole, exports more than it imports it is running a:

    A) Trade deficit
    B) Trading advantage
    C) Trade surplus
    D) Trading disadvantage
    E) None of the above

13) When a country, as a whole, imports more than it exports it is running a:

    A) Trade deficit
    B) Trade balance
    C) Trade surplus
    D) Beneficial trade status
    E) None of the above

14) When a country at the end of its fiscal year has money left over, it has a:

    A) Budget deficit
    B) Budget miracle
    C) Budget currency
    D) Budget surplus
    E) None of the above

16) When a country has to borrow to meet its fiscal obligation for the current year, it is running a:

    A) Budget discrepancy
    B) Budget shortfall
    C) Budget surplus
    D) Budget deficit
    E) None of the above

16) A country which has a favorable interest rate environment should have, relative to other countries:

    A) Lower interest rates
    B) Relatively equal interest rates
    C) Higher interest rates
    D) Significantly lower interest rates
    E) None of the above

17) Currency represents a specific countries:

    A) Interest rates
    B) Country stock market
    C) Unit of money
    D) Unit of economic productivity
    E) None of the above

18) Most countries have a major banking entity that regulates that countries banking industry and monetary policy, these entities are referred to as:

    A) Bank supervisory units
    B) Bank regulatory operators
    C) Banking commissions
    D) Central banks
    E) None of the above

Chapter 9 Review Course

1) An option is a:

   A) Derivative
   B) High risk investment
   C) Right to buy or sell a security
   D) Short-term security (generally)
   E) All of the above

2) The right to purchase a security is called a:

   A) Put
   B) Call
   C) Stake
   D) Lot
   E) None of the above

3) The right to sell a security is called:

   A) Put
   B) Call
   C) Stake
   D) Lot
   E) None of the above

4) Which of the following is not a component of stock option pricing:

   A) Time to expiration
   B) Underlying security's price
   C) Underlying security's Beta
   D) Interest rates
   E) None of the above

5) The body which has regulatory and administrative oversight of the option market is:

   A) The Options Supervisory Board
   B) The Options Regulatory Agency
   C) The Securities and Exchange Commission
   D) The Options Clearing Corporation
   E) None of the above

Chapter 10 Review Course

1) A retirement account which receives "special" tax considerations is termed a:

    A) Retirement plan
    B) IRA
    C) Pension plan
    D) Qualified plan
    E) None of the above

2) Which of the following does not apply to an IRA:

    A) Maximum per year contribution of $3,000.00 per individual
    B) Maximum per year contribution of $6,000.00 per married couple
    C) Tax penalty if withdrawals before age 59 ½
    D) Deferred tax treatment
    E) Never a mandatory withdrawal
    F) None of the above

3) Which investment would not be allowed in an IRA:

    A) Stock
    B) Bonds
    C) Mutual funds
    D) Annuities
    E) None of the above

4) Of the following, which investment would be allowed in an IRA:

    A) Cash value insurance policies
    B) Term insurance
    C) Art and collectibles
    D) Unit trusts
    E) None of the above

5) The company which actually "holds" the IRA is called the:
    A) Protector
    B) Custodian
    C) Company of Record
    D) Registrar
    E) None of the above

6) When moving money directly from one IRA to another IRA you have completed:

    A) Direct Transfer
    B) Money transfer
    C) Rollover
    D) Direct rollover
    E) None of the above

7) When moving money out of a Pension plan and directly into an IRA, you have completed a:

    A) Direct transfer
    B) Rollover
    C) Direct rollover
    D) Money transfer
    E) None of the above

8) When you withdraw money out of any qualified plan, deposit the money in your bank account, and within 60 days redeposit the funds into an IRA, you have completed a:

    A) Direct transfer
    B) Rollover
    C) Direct rollover
    D) Money transfer
    E) None of the above

9) Which of the following is not a ROTH IRA characteristic:

    A) Tax deferred treatment
    B) $3,000.00 maximum contribution
    C) Tax free withdrawal after age 59 ½
    D) Non-penalty withdrawal any time
    E) None of the above

10) Keogh plans were designed to provide retirement benefits primarily for:

    A) Women
    B) Senior citizens
    C) Non-profit organizations
    D) Self-employed persons
    E) None of the above

11) Which is not a type of corporate pension plan:

    A)   Defined Contribution plan
    B)   Money Purchase plan
    C)   Defined Benefit
    D)   Unfunded Pension Liability
    E)   None of the above

12) Retirement plans set up primarily for employees of non-profit organizations are:

    A)   401-K plans
    B)   403-B plans
    C)   404-A plans
    D)   408-N plans
    E)   None of the above

13) The most common type of corporate sponsored retirement plan is the:

    A)   IRA
    B)   Keogh
    C)   401-K
    D)   Profit Sharing plan
    E)   None of the above

14) The program designed primarily for small employers is:

    A)   SEP IRA
    B)   IRA
    C)   401-K
    D)   SAR SEP
    E)   None of the above

Chapter 11 Review Course

1) Which of the following is a Self Regulatory Organization?

    A) New York Stock Exchange
    B) National Association of Securities Dealers
    C) Chicago Board of Options Exchange
    D) Pacific Stock Exchange
    E) All of the above

2) The primary functions of a Self Regulatory Organization are?

    A) To promote the organization
    B) To regulate the organization
    C) To adjudicate the organization
    D) All of the above
    E) None of the above

3) Self Regulatory Organizations are:

    A) Social organizations
    B) Political Organizations
    C) Trade Organizations
    D) None of the above

4) Self Regulatory Organizations have the power to:

    A) Fine
    B) Censure
    C) Suspend
    D) Imprison
    E) All of the above
    F) None of the above
    G) A, B, and C only

Answers and Explanations
Chapter 1

1) C. When an investor purchases common stock, the investor is purchasing an "ownership" interest in the corporation.

2) B The term "Equity securities" encompasses stocks, warrants, rights, and ADRs.

3) C Outstanding shares are issued shares currently in the public marketplace.

4) D All of the listed are rights afforded to common shareholders.

5) D A proxy is a document resembling a card or form, which details the corporate actions to be discussed and voted upon during the annual meeting. This form allows for the vote to be cast, and then returned to the corporation for recording. It is similar to casting an "absantee" ballot in a public election.

6) C Wall Street, is sometimes referred to as "the street", meaning all brokerage firms on Wall Street. Therefore, the shares are held in "street name" referring to the brokerage firms name.

7) D The transfer agent is responsible for executing all of the listed functions.

8) D When a corporation distributes a portion of its net profits to shareholders, it is referred to as a dividend payment.

9) E All of the listed are characteristics of American Depository Receipts.

10) D A debenture is a type of bond, which of course is a fixed income or debt security.

11) D While preferred stock prices do not fluctuate nearly as much as common stock prices, they do fluctuate.

12) D All of the terms listed represent different characteristics of preferred stocks.

Answers and Explanations
Chapter 2

1) D   Bonds are a fixed income security, also referred to as debt securities.

2) B   All of the listed with the exception of individuals, issue bonds.

3) E   All "book entry" securities, stocks or bonds, are recorded only in
computer databases. There is no physical certificate of ownership.

4) C   Another term for the coupon is "coupon rate", both represent the
amount of interest stated on the bond at issuance.

5) A   The term "zero" should provide the reader with a valuable clue.
Since we know from the above question that the "coupon" represents
the interest, then it follows that a "zero-coupon" would pay no interest.

6) E   Its easy if you just remember, bonds and interest rates have an **inverse**
relationship.

7) C   Absolute yield has no relevant meaning, but all of the other yields are extremely
important for bond investors.

8) E   Other than maturity risk, all others listed represent significant types of bond risk.
There is no such thing as a "maturity" risk

9) A   The federal government is by far, the largest issuer of bonds.

10) C   A treasury bill has a maturity of 1 year of less, treasury note 1 to ten years,
and treasury bond, 10 to 30 years.

11) A   The government allows certain firms to buy the issued bonds, then resell these
securities to all other customers, both individual and corporate.

12) D   All bonds issued by state and local governments are called municipal bonds.

13) D   The person possessing the bonds actually clips pieces of paper (Interest Coupons)
from the bond and remits them to the appropriate authority for payment. There
is no check of identification, whoever is in possession of the bonds…..is paid.

14) D   A, B, and C are all types of municipal bonds. There is no such thing as a
"city bond".

15) A   The holder of municipal bonds are not required to pay federal taxes on the interest received. This tax break was granted by congress as an incentive for private investment in local and state governments.

16) C   Many municipal bonds are also tax exempt from local and state taxation if the purchaser resides in the state where the bonds were issued.

17) D   Investors should be able to understand all the effects taxation may have on bond interest payments.

18) A   Treasury Bills are any Treasury issued security with a maturity of one year or less.

19) B   Treasury Notes are any Treasury issued security with a maturity of not more than 10 years, and not less than 1 year.

20) C   Treasury Bonds are any Treasury issued security with a maturity of not more than 30 years, and not less than 10 years.

21) C   The review by the attorney is called a "legal opinion".

22) B   An unqualified opinion means the attorney found no faults with the new issue. However, if the attorney had some concerns, they would be detailed in written form. In this case, the opinion rendered by the attorney would be called, "qualified".

23) B   Municipal bond trading is very light, at least in comparison with other types of bonds. By contrast, trading in corporate and Treasury bonds is quite heavy.

Answers and Explanations
Chapter 3

1) D   Money market securities are comprised of short term debt securities. Debt securities, are of course, fixed income securities.

2) C   All money market instruments mature in 1 year or less. The original maturities may be any length of time, but the current maturity must be 1 year or less to be considered a money market security.

3) D   All are true of money market instruments.

4) F   All of the listed securities can be money market instruments, are long as the time left to maturity is less than 1 year.

5) A   Money market securities generally consist of very safe individual securities, such as short term government securities or other highly rated, sometimes insured short term securities.

Answers and Explanations
Chapter 4

1) C   In 1940 congress passed the Investment Company Act which created three types of categories of investment companies. One of the three was termed "management companies", what we know today as mutual funds.

2) B   "Open end" and "closed end" are the twp primary categories of mutual funds.

3) D   The number of open end outstanding shares is always changing due to the constant purchases and redemptions of the shares. They generally have no limit on the number of outstanding, therefore, theoretically the number is unlimited.

4) D   Closed end funds can not have an unlimited number of outstanding shares, they have a finite number of shares which is specified at the time of issuance. The number can, however, be modified at the discretion of the board of directors, but it remains a finite number. The number of outstanding shares does not fluctuate from day to day as they do for open end funds.

5) D   Companies such as Charles Schwab, Merril Lynch, Fidelity are just a few who have issued proprietory mutual funds, and as such would be called the funds' sponsor.

6) C   The prospectus is the document which details all specifics of the fund, and is required by law to be available to the public.

7) C   All investments have some amount of risk. Usually, the more risk an investor is assuming, the higher the rate of interest paid to the investor. (If you should find a "riskless" investment, please apprise the author immediately.)

8) E   All of the listed examples are types of mutual funds.

9) B   Open end funds are purchased from and redeemed by the fund sponsor or an intermediary such as a brokerage firm. They do not trade on exchanges.

10) A   Closed end funds trade on exchanges just like regular stocks.

11) B   Funds which charge a sales fee are said to have an extra "load" to bear, namely the sales fee. From this analogy the term "loaded fund" came into existence and has become today common terminology.

12) A   Mutual funds which have no sales fees are referred to as "no-load" funds.

13) D   Net Asset Value is the mechanism used for the pricing of all open end funds. It represents the total closing values of the funds holdings divided by the total number of shares outstanding.

14) A   Because closed end funds trade on exchanges just like stocks, an investor knows immediately what price he or she will pay for a particular fund.

15) E   When you purchase an open end fund, typically you are purchasing at the current days closing price, however, sometimes brokerage firms have "cut-off" times for purchases just as banks have for deposits. Therefore, if your purchase or sell order is placed after the cut-off time, the investor will receive the closing price for the next business day.

16) D   While Merril Lynch does sponsor mutual funds, they also have many other types of business such as brokerage operations and investment banking divisions.

17) C   Large mutual fund companies such as Fidelity and Vangaurd, offer many different types of funds, the aggregate of these funds are termed fund families.

18) D   All except plant and equipment are normal operating fees associated with running a mutual fund company.

Answers and Explanations
Chapter 5

1) C   All securities, other than those being first introduced as an IPO, trade in the secondary market.

2) F   Stocks listed on the New York Stock Exchange are trading in the "first market". Because those same securities are not IPO stocks, they are also trading in the Secondary market, therefore, F would be the most correct answer.

3) A   A stock that is issued as an IPO, is said to trade in the "primary" market for the purpose of the IPO only, thereafter, it will trade in the secondary market.

4) B   Any existing security is trading in the secondary market.

5) C   Any security trading on the NASD is trading in the OTC market. The OTC market by definition is the second market.

6) E   Listed securities trading off-the-floor of the primary exchange is trading in the third market.

7) A   A specialist works for an exchange and performs certain duties which are designed to keep an "orderly" market.

8) A   Firms which only execute trades for "others", are termed "brokers".

9) C   Firms which execute trades for "itself", meaning its own internal accounts only, is called a Dealer. Firms which transact business for themselves and others are said to be acting as broker and dealer.

10) C   When a firm only executes trades for clients through other brokers the fee charged is called a commission.

11) A   When a firm executes trades out of its own inventory, the fee charged is termed a mark-up.

12) B   The market maker performs many of the same duties of the specialist, the primary difference is the specialist works on an exchange, and the market maker works off the exchange in the OTC market.

13) B   A market order is a directive to your broker to buy the stock immediately at the current prevailing price.

14) C   When placing an order at a specific price, the order is termed a limit order.

15) C An order to sell a security below the current price is a stop order. You are basically instructing the broker to "stop your losses" at a specific price.

16) C A day order expires after the current trading session.

17) D A GTC "good-til-cancelled" order, will remain in force until it executes, or until it is cancelled.

18) F This type of order is generally termed market at open, however, a market order would serve the same function.

19) E An order to buy or sell at any price at the end of the day is called a "market-on-close" order, therefore E is the correct answer.

20) C A short sell, is an action that might be taken if an investor believes the stock in question is going to decline in price in the near future.

21) A Full service firms are typically firms that give advice to clients, and help assist in the development of the clients' investment strategy.

22) D Discount firms typically do not give investment advice. Because of this, they have traditionally charged lower transaction fees, and hence have become known as "discount" brokerage firms.

23) D Deep discount brokerage firms are the offspring of discount brokerage firms. They offer fewer services and charge much lower transaction fees.

Answers and Explanations
Chapter 6

1) C   When an investor purchases securities on margin, the investor is using the funds they have in their account and borrowing the remainder from the brokerage firm.

2) D   All securities purchased on margin are registered in the name of the brokerage firm, which is also referred to as "street name".

3) D   The amount "loaned" to the investor is the amount that must be repaid, however, the correct term used to describe the amount of "loaned funds" is "debit balance", therefore, D is the correct answer, not B.

4) C   All margin calculations begin with the total value of securities in the margin account. This value is called "current market value", its called current because the figure generally changes from day to day.

5) D   As the debit balance is the amount "loaned" by the brokerage firm, the "equity" is the amount not loaned by the brokerage firm. The equity represents that portion of the total account value that is owned by the account holder.

6) C   The rules and regulations governing margin loan rates is referred to as "Regulation T".

7) C   Once the investor has met the initial requirements of purchasing on margin, any subsequent request for funds is referred to as a "Maintenance Call or House Call".

8) B   The additional amount securities which can be bought using margin is called "buying power".

9) D   Regulation T requires a minimum account value of $2,000.00 before the account holder can utilize margin capabilities.

Answers and Explanations
Chapter 7

1) D Securities professionals use various methods of analysis in an attempt to quantify and reduce risk.

2) D Systematic and market risk are types of general risks which affect the overall market.

3) E Conversely, risks that primarily affect one specific security are referred to as unsystematic risk and business risk.

4) C Fundamental analysis seeks to answer the question of "which" security to purchase.

5) D Statement of retained assets is not a recognized financial statement.

6) D Net worth represents the value after all debts are paid.

7) D Working capital is what corporations use to conduct ongoing operations, therefore it's logical to take readily available assets (currents assets) and subtract debts which must be paid soon (currents liabilities), to arrive at a figure which represents what is available for the corporation to utilize for continuing operations. (working capital)

8) D Book value represents the value of the entity after all assets are sold and all debts have been paid.

9) A Profit margins are a percentage figure which is stated in relation to the corporations sales.

10) D Return on assets, although stated as a percentage, is a measure of the income the corporation receives in relation to its total assets.

11) D Cash flow measures how much "cash" the corporation has to pay for ongoing operations.

12) D This is fairly straight forward, earnings per share measures earnings on a per "common" share basis.

13) B Technical analyst use charts very often in their analyses, because of this, they are often called "chartist".

14) C   A security whose price continues to rise over a period of time is said to be in an uptrend.

15) C   A security whose price continues to move down, is in a downtrend.

16) D   A security moving markedly above or below its trading range is termed a "breakout".

17) D   A moving average adds new points to the end of the measurement, and subtracts old point from the beginning of the measurement.

18) D   Much like a sports team, a stock or market moving strongly is said to have momentum, yes, the big "mo".

19) D   Beta allows investors to judge the risk of certain securities, as compared to the overall market and thereby enables investors to assume more or less risk to fit their individual risk tolerance.

Answers and Explanations
Chapter 8

1) E   While depressions do occur from time to time, it is not a recognized
        phase of the business cycle, all other choices are recognized phases.

2) A   Economic policies enacted by legislatures are examples of fiscal policy.

3) B   Monetary policies are policies which effect the supply of "money" in the
        economy. The Federal Reserve has total control of raising or lowering
        interest rates, therefore, any action by the Federal Reserve would be
        an act of monetary policy.

4) D   Rising prices are generally referred to as inflation.

5) D   When prices fall for no apparent reason, the economy is experiencing "deflation".

6) D   The Consumer Price Index, seeks to measure the prices of goods and services which
        individuals (consumers) are subject to purchase.

7) D   The Producer Price Index seeks to measure the prices of goods and services which
        are primarily purchased by businesses.

8) A   Since inflation reduces purchasing power, its rate must be subtracted to arrive
        at the "real" interest rate.

9) D   The discount rate is the rate which affects the pocketbooks of average consumers
        the most. Mortgage rates, car loans, personal loans, and business loans are all
        tied to the discount rate.

10) E   All functions listed are responsibilities of the Federal Reserve.

11) D   There is no such thing as adjunct indicators.

12) C   When a country exports more than it imports, more money is entering the
         country than leaving the country. This occurrence is called a trade surplus.

13) A   When a country is importing more than it's exporting, the country is sending out more
         money than its receiving. The occurrence is called a trade deficit.

14) D   When any entity has money remaining after meeting its financial obligations, it
         has a surplus. Because this question refers to a country, and all countries
         operate on budgets, this surplus is called a "budget" surplus.

15) D   A country operates in many ways just like a family. When it has financial obligations to meet and its money is gone, it must borrow to meet those remaining obligations.

16) C   If the country has higher interest rates relative to other countries, capital will flow into the country, stimulating security prices and currency prices.

17) C   All countries have their own money, another word for money is currency.

18) D   Central banks regulate the banking operations and monetary policy of their specific country.

Answers and Explanations
Chapter 9

1) E   All of the items listed are features of options.

2) B   An option which allows an investor to purchase the underlying security, is termed a "call".

3) A   An option which allows an investor to sell the underlying security is termed a "put".

4) D   While interest rates, and their future direction, would have a impact on the pricing of bond options, they have very little if any impact on stock options.

5) D   The Options Clearing corporation is the regulatory body which governs the options market.

Answers and Explanations
Chapter 10

1) D   There are many types of retirement accounts, but those that receive special IRS tax treatment are called "qualified" retirement accounts.

2) E   IRA's require a mandatory distribution after the age of 70 ½. The amount of the mandatory distribution varies according to the individual.

3) E   All of the listed investment are allowed in an IRA.

4) D   Unit trust are allowed in IRA accounts, however, all others listed are prohibited.

5) B   Any company which holds the actual IRA is called the "custodian". It's usually a financial institution such as a bank, insurance company or brokerage firm.

6) A   A direct transfer occurs when money transfers from one institution to another without the individual taking possession of the funds.

7) C   A direct rollover occurs when money is transferred from a "non" IRA qualified plan, (pension plan, 401-K plan, etc) to an IRA without the individual even taking possession of funds

8) B   A rollover occurs when the individual takes possession of the money, (distribution from non IRA qualified plan) then subsequently deposits the money into an IRA within the 60 day time allowance.

9) D   A ROTH IRA does allow distributions without penalties, but only for specific reasons. (Also, ROTH "contributions", not gains, can always be withdrawn without penalty)

10) D   Keogh's were designed specifically for self employed individuals. They are often used by doctors, lawyers, and other self employed professionals.

11) E   All of the options listed are types of corporate pension plans.

12) B   403-B plans are very similar to 401-K plans, however they were designed specifically for "non profit" organizations.

13) C   The 401-K is by far the most popular and common type of corporate sponsored pension plan.

14) D   The SAR SEP was designed to give small employers the ability to offer their workforce retirement benefits similar to those of larger corporations. Only employers with 25 or fewer employees can utilize a SARSEP plan.

Answers and Explanations
Chapter 11

1) E   All of the listed organizations are Self Regulatory Organizations. As their name implies, they "self – regulate" their organization.

2) D   SRO's perform all of the duties listed.

3) D   SRO's are "Trade Associations", not trade "organizations".

4) G   Self Regulatory Organizations can fine, censure, and suspend, but they cannot put a person in jail.